Y0-BYV-765

The Love and Kisses
Quote Book

Also by
Allen Klein

The Celebrate-Your-Life Quote Book

The Change-Your-Life Quote Book

The Lift-Your-Spirits Quote Book

The Simplify-Your-Life Quote Book

Up Words for Down Days

The Wise and Witty Quote Book

The Love and Kisses
Quote Book

500 QUOTATIONS TO SNUGGLE UP TO

Compiled by **Allen Klein**

GRAMERCY BOOKS
NEW YORK

Copyright © 2006 by Allen Klein

All rights reserved under International and Pan-American Copyright Conventions.

No part of this book may be reproduced or transmitted in any form or by any means electronic or mechanical including photocopying and recording, or by any information storage and retrieval system, without permission in writing from the publisher.

Published by Gramercy Books, an imprint of Random House Value Publishing, a division of Random House, Inc., New York.

Gramercy is a registered trademark and the colophon is a trademark of Random House, Inc.

Random House
New York • Toronto • London • Sydney • Auckland
www.randomhouse.com

Printed and bound in Singapore

A catalog record for this title is available from the Library of Congress.

0-517-22463-1

My gratitude and love
to the higher power who gave me talent
and to all those along my path
who helped nourish it.

CONTENTS

INTRODUCTION

One of the founders of the *Saturday Review of Literature,* Christopher Morley, once noted "If we all discovered that we had only five minutes left to say all that we wanted to say, every telephone booth would be occupied by people calling other people to tell them that they loved them."

This book is a reminder not to wait for those last moments.

Nearly all of these more than 500 quotations, about first love through unconditional love, illustrate just how powerful love can be. These insights can help bring more love to every aspect of your life or someone else's.

While compiling these quotations, their wisdom kept ringing in my ears and opened me up to both giving and receiving more love. I hope the words in this book do the same for you.

ALLEN KLEIN,
SAN FRANCISCO

To speak of love is to make love.

HONORÉ DE BALZAC

Love Makes the World Go 'Round

What is Love?

Love doesn't make the world go 'round.
Love is what makes the ride worthwhile.

FRANKLIN P. JONES

Love is the master key
which opens the gates of happiness.

OLIVER WENDELL HOLMES

Love is heaven and heaven is love.

WALTER SCOTT

Love should be a tree whose roots are deep in the earth,
but whose branches extend into heaven.

BERTRAND RUSSELL

Love is patient, love is kind. It does not envy, it does not boast,
it is not proud. It is not rude, it is not self-seeking, it is not
easily angered, it keeps no record of wrongs. Love does not
delight in evil but rejoices with the truth. It always protects,
always trusts, always hopes, always perseveres.

1 CORINTHIANS 13:4-7

Love is never lost. If not reciprocated it will flow back
and soften and purify the heart.

WASHINGTON IRVING

Love is what we were born with.
Fear is what we learned here.

MARIANNE WILLIAMSON

Love has no limits. Love never ends.
Love is reborn and reborn and reborn.

THICH NHAT HANH

Love has no age, as it is always renewing.

BLAISE PASCAL

Love is like infinity: You can't have more or less infinity, and
you can't compare two things to see if they're "equally infinite."
Infinity just is, and that's the way I think love is, too.

FRED ROGERS

Love is an energy—it can neither be created nor destroyed.
It just is and always will be, giving meaning to life
and direction to goodness....
Love will never die.

BRYCE COURTNEY

Love is the immortal flow of energy that nourishes,
extends and preserves. Its eternal goal is life.

SMILEY BLANTON

Love is a mighty power, a great and complete good.
Love alone lightens every burden,
and makes the rough places smooth.

THOMAS À KEMPIS

Without love our life is…a ship without a rudder…
like a body without a soul.

SHOLOM ALEICHEM

I define love thus: the will to extend one's self for the
purpose of nurturing one's own or another's spiritual growth.

M. SCOTT PECK

The essence of love is creative companionship,
the fulfillment of one life by another.

JOHN ERSKINE

Love is but the discovery of ourselves in others,
and the delight in the recognition.

ALEXANDER SMITH

Love is the experience of others as "us,"
and not separately as him, her or them.

KEN KEYES, JR.

Love is a game that two can play and both win.

EVA GABOR

Love is the only game
that is not called on account of darkness.

ANONYMOUS

When the satisfaction or security of another person becomes
as significant to one as is one's own satisfaction or security,
then the state of love exists.

HARRY STACK SULLIVAN

A lady of forty-seven who has been married twenty-seven years
and has six children knows what love really is
and once described it for me like this:
"Love is what you've been through with somebody."

JAMES THURBER

Love is when I am concerned
with your relationship with your own life
rather than with your relationship to mine.

STEWART EMORY

Love is...the ability and willingness to allow those that you
care for to be what they choose for themselves,
without any insistence that they satisfy you.

WAYNE DYER

Love is an act of endless forgiveness,
a tender look which becomes a habit.

PETER USTINOV

Love is the free exercise of choice. Two people love each
other only when they are quite capable of living without each
other but choose to live with each other.

M. SCOTT PECK

Love is when two people
who care for each other get confused.

BOB SCHNEIDER

What is irritating about love is that
it is a crime that requires an accomplice.

CHARLES BAUDELAIRE

Love is said to be blind, but I know lots of fellows in love
who can see twice as much in their sweethearts as I can.

JOSH BILLINGS

Love is not blind—it sees more, not less.
But because it sees more,
it is willing to see less.

JULIUS GORDEN

Love is like quicksilver in the hand.
Leave the fingers open, and it stays. Clutch it, and it darts away.

DOROTHY PARKER

Love is always open arms. If you close your arms about love
you will find that you are left holding only yourself.

LEO BUSCAGLIA

Love is the irresistible desire
to be irresistibly desired.

ROBERT FROST

Love is the same as like except you feel sexier.

JUDITH VIORST

Love is, above all, the gift of oneself.

JEAN ANOUILH

Love is like an hourglass,
with the heart filling up as the brain empties.

JULES RENARD

Love is an infusion of intense feeling, a fine madness
that makes you drunk, and when one is in love, life can be
a succession of free falls while working without a net.

MERLE SHAIN

Love is friendship set on fire.

JEREMY TAYLOR

**Love is a fire. But whether it is going to warm your hearth
or burn down your house, you can never tell.**

JOAN CRAWFORD

**What a silly thing love is! It is not half as useful as logic,
for it does not prove anything and it is always telling
one things that are not going to happen, and
making one believe things that are not true.**

OSCAR WILDE

**Love is an endless mystery,
for it has nothing else to explain it.**

RABINDRANATH TAGORE

Love is a mystery which, when solved, evaporates.

NED ROREN

Love is much nicer to be in than an automobile accident,
a tight girdle, a higher tax bracket or
a holding pattern over Philadelphia.

JUDITH VIORST

If love is the answer,
could you rephrase the question?

LILY TOMLIN

I know what love is: Tracy and Hepburn, Bogart and Bacall,
Romeo and Juliet, Jackie and John and Marilyn.

IAN SHOALES

Everyone admits that love is wonderful and necessary,
yet no one can agree on what it is.

DIANE ACKERMAN

Love betters what is best.

WILLIAM WORDSWORTH

Love conceals all of one's faults.

ITALIAN PROVERB

**Love often makes a fool of the cleverest man,
and as often gives cleverness to the most foolish.**

FRENCH PROVERB

**Love seeks one thing only: The good of the one loved.
It leaves all the other secondary effects to take care of
themselves. Love, therefore, is its own reward.**

THOMAS MERTON

Love understands love: it needs no talk.

FRANCES R. HAVERGAL

**Love feels no burden, thinks nothing of trouble
and attempts what is above its strength.**

THOMAS À KEMPIS

**To love someone deeply gives you strength.
Being loved by someone deeply gives you courage.**

LAO-TZU

Life has taught us that love does not consist in gazing at
each other but in looking outward together
in the same direction.

ANTOINE DE SAINT EXUPÉRY

We are shaped and fashioned by what we love.

JOHANN WOLFGANG VON GOETHE

To love is to suffer. To avoid suffering one must not love. But
then one suffers from not loving. Therefore to love is to suffer,
not to love is to suffer. To suffer is to suffer. To be happy is to
love. To be happy then is to suffer. But suffering makes one
unhappy. Therefore, to be unhappy one must love, or love to
suffer, or suffer from too much happiness. I hope you're getting
this down.

WOODY ALLEN

Without love the world itself would not survive.

LOPE DE VEGA

Love cannot save life from death;
but it can fulfill life's purpose.

ARNOLD TOYNBEE

Paradise is always where love dwells.

JEAN PAUL RICHTER

Only through love can we attain to communion with God.

ALBERT SCHWEITZER

In our life there is a single color, as on an artist's palette, which provides the meaning of life and art. It is the color of love.

MARC CHAGALL

Love is something eternal; the aspect may change, but not the essence.

VINCENT VAN GOGH

Love is a canvas furnished by Nature and embroidered by imagination.

VOLTAIRE

Love is the only gold.

ALFRED, LORD TENNYSON

There is nothing in the world as sweet as love.

What does love look like? It has the hands to help others. It has the feet to hasten to the poor and needy. It has eyes to see misery and want. It has the ears to hear the sighs and sorrows of men. That is what love looks like.

SAINT AUGUSTINE

Harmony is pure love, for love is a concerto.

LOPE DE VEGA

Love is friendship set to music.

E. JOSEPH CROSSMANN

Love is like a violin. The music may stop now and then, but the strings remain forever.

JUNE MASTERS BACHER

Love is a letter on pink stationary.

CHARLES SCHULZ

What is love? It is the morning and the evening star.

SINCLAIR LEWIS

Love is the light you can see by.

BESS STREETER ALDRICH

Love is the poetry of the senses.

HONORÉ DE BALZAC

Love is the greatest beautifier in the universe.

MAY CHRISTIE

Love is no hot-house flower, but a wild plant, born of a wet night, born of an hour of sunshine; sprung from wild seed, blown along the road by a wild wind.

JOHN GALSWORTHY

Life is the flower for which love is the honey.

VICTOR HUGO

Love is a fruit in season at all times, and in reach of every hand.

MOTHER TERESA

Love is the greatest refreshment in life.

PABLO PICASSO

Love is the food of the universe. It is the most important ingredient in life. Children go towards love, they thrive on love and grow on love, and would die without it.

SANAYA ROMAN

Love is sharing your popcorn.

CHARLES SCHULZ

Love, like a chicken salad or restaurant hash, must be taken with blind faith or it loses its flavor.

HELEN ROWLAND

Love is sweet, but tastes better with bread.

YIDDISH PROVERB

Love Is a Many-Splendored Thing

Falling in Love

To love and be loved
is to feel the sun from both sides.

DAVID VISCOTT

You'll never be happy if you can't figure out that loving people is all there is. And that it's more important to love than be loved. Because that is when you feel love, by loving somebody.

GWYNETH PALTROW

The simple but observable fact is that the more you love, the more you are able to love.

JOYCE BROTHERS

Love, and you shall be loved.

RALPH WALDO EMERSON

Love is not getting, but giving. It is sacrifice. And sacrifice is glorious! I have no patience with women who measure and weigh their love like a country doctor dispensing capsules. If a man is worth loving at all, he is worth loving generously, even recklessly.

MARIE DRESSLER

If you give your life as a wholehearted response to love, then love will wholeheartedly respond to you.

MARIANNE WILLIAMSON

The one thing we never give enough of is love.

HENRY MILLER

Saving love doesn't bring any interest.

MAE WEST

**Only love can be divided endlessly
and still not diminish.**

ANNE MORROW LINDBERGH

**You can offer your love completely to hundreds of people
and still retain the same love you had originally. It is like
knowledge. The wise man can teach all he knows and when
he's through he'll still know all that he has taught.**

LEO BUSCAGLIA

I know of only one duty, and that is to love.

ALBERT CAMUS

There is more pleasure in loving
than in being loved.

THOMAS FULLER

All that we deeply love becomes a part of us.

HELEN KELLER

Tell me whom you love, and I will tell you what you are.

ARSÉNE HOUSSAYE

Listen to no one who tells you how to love. Your love is like
no other, and that is what makes it beautiful.

PAUL WILLIAMS

We waste time looking for the perfect lover,
instead of creating the perfect love.

TOM ROBBINS

You will find as you look back upon your life that the
moments when you have truly lived are the moments when
you have done things in the spirit of love.

HENRY DRUMMOND

**You don't have to go looking for love
when it's where you come from.**

WERNER ERHARD

The love we desire is already within us.

A COURSE IN MIRACLES

**When you really want love
you will find it waiting for you.**

OSCAR WILDE

**When love comes it comes without effort,
like perfect weather.**

HELEN YGLESIAS

**We can never at any time absorb more love
than we're ready for.**

MAGNON MCLAUGHLIN

I think that when we look for love courageously,
it reveals itself, and we wind up attracting even more love.
If one person really wants us, everyone does.
But if we're alone, we become even more alone.

PAULO COELHO

The supreme happiness in life
is the conviction that we are loved.

VICTOR HUGO

If you ever expect to be loved,
you must reveal who you are.

LEO BUSCAGLIA

Love doesn't drop on you unexpectedly; you have to give off
signals, sort of like an amateur radio operator.

HELEN GURLEY BROWN

To love is to receive a glimpse of heaven.

KAREN SUNDE

There is no surprise more magical than the surprise of being in love. It is God's finger on man's shoulder.

CHARLES MORGAN

We want to be rich, to be admired, to eat like a horse and be skinny as a snake. To have small children ask for our autographs, to be on terrific medications that make us calm and witty and sexy. To sing Irving Berlin and Gershwin and Porter at the Oak Room and be described in the Times as "luminous." But in the absence of all that, it's enough to be loved.

GARRISON KEILLOR

To be loved, be lovable.

OVID

When love is good it can make you fly.
Winning it is worth the risk.
People fall in love and glow for weeks.

GEORGE DAVIS

Gravitation can not be held responsible
for people falling in love.

ALBERT EINSTEIN

Falling in love consists merely
in uncorking the imagination
and bottling the common sense.

HELEN ROWLAND

To fall in love you have to be in the state of mind
for it to take, like a disease.

NANCY MITFORD

To be in love is merely to be in a state of perceptual anesthesia—
to mistake an ordinary young man for a Greek god
or an ordinary young woman for a goddess.

H. L. MENCKEN

Romantic love is mental illness.
But it's a pleasurable one.

FRAN LEBOWITZ

It is difficult to know at what moment love begins;
it is less difficult to know that it has begun.

HENRY WADSWORTH LONGFELLOW

A guy knows he's in love when he loses
interest in his car for a couple of days.

TIM ALLEN

Love doesn't just sit there, like a stone; it has to be made,
like bread, remade all the time, made new.

URSULA LEGUIN

A successful marriage requires falling in love many times,
always with the same person.

GERMAINE GREER

Any time that is not spent on love is wasted.

TORQUATO TASSO

There is always something left to love.
And if you ain't learned that, you ain't learned nothing.

LORRAINE HANSBERRY

Love affairs are the only real education in life.

MARLENE DIETRICH

There is no remedy for love but to love more.

HENRY DAVID THOREAU

That is the true season of love, when we believe that we
alone can love, that no one could ever have loved so before
us and that no one will love in the same way after us.

JOHANN WOLFGANG VON GOETHE

The weather is always fair when people are in love.

ITALIAN PROVERB

I was nauseous and tingly all over.
I was either in love or I had smallpox.

WOODY ALLEN

To fall in love is awfully simple,
but to fall out of love is simply awful.

One does not fall "in" or "out" of love.
One grows in love.

LEO BUSCAGLIA

Being in love is experiencing a person's essence
and expression of that essence, and being unwilling
for the other person not to express it.

STEWART EMORY

The meeting of two personalities is like
the contact of two chemical substances:
if there is any reaction, both are transformed.

CARL JUNG

There is no disguise which can hide love for long where it exists,
or simulate it where it does not.

FRANÇOIS DUC DE LA ROCHEFOUCAULD

Where love does not exist, plant it and it will grow.

SAN JUAN DE LA CRUZ

It doesn't matter who you love or how you love,
but that you love.

ROD McKUEN

Hello Young Lovers

First Love

First romance, first love, is something so special to all of us, both emotionally and physically, that it touches our lives and enriches them forever.

ROSEMARY ROGERS

One always returns to one's first loves.

HENRI ÉTIENNE

How on earth are you ever going to explain in terms of chemistry and physics so important a biological phenomenon as first love?

ALBERT EINSTEIN

Love is so very timid when 'tis new.

LORD BYRON

The magic of first love is our ignorance that it can ever end.

BENJAMIN DISRAELI

Sensual pleasures have the fleeting brilliance of a comet; a happy marriage has the tranquillity of a lovely sunset.

ANN LANDERS

The first sigh of love is the last of wisdom.

ANTOINE BRET

We are all mortal until the first kiss
and the second glass of wine.

EDUARDO GALEANO

How delicious is the winning of a kiss at love's beginning.

THOMAS CAMPBELL

There's nothing half so sweet in life as love's young dream.

CLEMENT C. MOORE

First love is only a little foolishness and a lot of curiosity.

GEORGE BERNARD SHAW

Young love needs dangers and barriers to nourish it.

GEORGE SAND

When a couple of young people strongly devoted to each other
commence to eat onions, it is safe to pronounce them engaged.

JAMES MONTGOMERY BAILEY

Teenagers don't know what love is. They have mixed-up ideas. They go for a drive, and the boy runs out of gas, and they smooch a little and the girl says she loves him. That isn't love. Love is when you are married twenty-five years, smooching in your living room, and he runs out of gas and she says she still loves him. That's love.

NORM CROSBY

Young love is a flame; very pretty, often very hot and fierce, but still only light and flickering. The love of the older and disciplined heart is as coals, deep-burning, unquenchable.

HENRY WARD BEECHER

The heart that loves is always young.

GREEK PROVERB

A boy's love comes from a full heart;
a man's is more often the result of a full stomach.

JEROME K. JEROME

Love and eggs are best when they are fresh.

RUSSIAN PROVERB

I Just Called to Say I Love You

Romantic Love

How do I love thee? Let me count the ways.
I love thee to the depth and breadth and height
My soul can reach

ELIZABETH BARRETT BROWNING

Brevity may be the soul of wit, but not when someone's saying "I love you." When someone's saying "I love you," he always ought to give a lot of details: Like, why does he love you? And, when and where did he first begin to love you? Favorable comparisons with all the other women he ever loved are also welcome. And even though he insists it would take forever to count the ways in which he loves you, let him start counting.

JUDITH VIORST

I love you as New Englanders love pie!

DON MARQUIS

I love thee like pudding; if thou wert pie, I'd eat thee.

JOHN RAY

I love you more than yesterday, less than tomorrow.

EDMOND ROSTAND

I love you no matter what you do,
but do you have to do so much of it?

JEAN ILLSLEY CLARKE

I love you, not for what you are,
but for what I am when I am with you.

ROY CROFT

If I know what love is, it is because of you.

HERMANN HESSE

All that I love loses half its pleasure
if you are not there to share it.

CLARA ORTEGA

All that you are, all that I owe to you, justifies my love,
and nothing, not even you, would keep me from adoring you.

MARQUIS DE LAFAYETTE

Ask the child why it is born; ask the flower why it blossoms,
ask the sun why it shines. I love you because I must love you.

GEORGE UPTON

"Love, shmove," Papa used to say,
"I love blintzes; did I marry one?"

SAM LEVENSON

It is a curious thought,
but it is only when you see people looking ridiculous
that you realize just how much you love them.

AGATHA CHRISTIE

In love the paradox occurs
that two beings become one and yet remain two.

ERICH FROMM

For one human being to love another; that is perhaps the
most difficult of all our tasks, the ultimate, the last test and
proof, the work for which all other work is but preparation.

RAINER MARIA RILKE

There is a universal truth that I have found in my work.
Everybody longs to be loved. And the greatest thing we can do
is let somebody know that they are loved and capable of loving.

FRED ROGERS

When one is truly in love,
one not only says it, but shows it.

HENRY WADSWORTH LONGFELLOW

We are told that people stay in love because of chemistry,
or because they remain intrigued with each other,
because of many kindnesses, because of luck.... But
part of it has got to be forgiveness and gratefulness.
The understanding that, so, you're no bargain,
but you love and you are loved. Anyway.

ELLEN GOODMAN

And what do all the great words come to in the end, but that?—
I love you—I am at rest with you—I have come home.

DOROTHY L. SAYERS

From the moment we walk out the door until
we come back home our sensibilities are so assaulted by
the world at large that we have to soak up as much love
as we can get, simply to arm ourselves. It's like going to the
gas station for a refill. We humans need to hear "I love you"
and we need to hear it as often as we can.

PATTY DUKE

The greatest weakness of most humans is their hesitancy to tell others how much they love them while they're still alive.

ORLANDO A. BATTISTA

In order to love simply,
it is necessary to know how to show love.

FYODOR DOSTOEVSKY

If you love somebody, tell them.

ROD McKUEN

Romance is the icing but love is the cake.

ANONYMOUS

Love is a valentine with lace all around the edges.

CHARLES SCHULZ

In a great romance,
each person plays a part the other really likes.

ELIZABETH ASHLEY

Romantic love is a passionate spiritual-emotional-sexual
attachment between a man and a woman that reflects a high
regard for the value of each other's person.

NATHANIEL BRANDEN

Story writers say that love is concerned only
with young people, and the excitement and glamour of
romance end at the altar. How blind they are. The best
romance is inside marriage; the finest love stories
come after the wedding, not before.

IRVING STONE

For a marriage to last it must be one long affair.

ANONYMOUS

Some people claim that marriage interferes with romance.
There's no doubt about it. Anytime you have a romance, your
wife is bound to interfere.

GROUCHO MARX

My wife is really sentimental. One Valentine's Day I gave her a ring, and to this day, she has never forgotten those three little words that were engraved inside—Made in Taiwan!

LEOPOLD FETCHNER

In real love you want the other person's good. In romantic love you want the other person.

MARGARET ANDERSON

There is nothing better for the spirit or the body than a love affair. It elevates the thoughts and flattens the stomachs.

BARBARA HOWER

It is only with the heart that one can see rightly: what is essential if invisible to the eye.

ANTOINE DE SAINT EXUPÉRY

The heart has reasons that reason does not understand.

JACQUES BÉNIGNE BOSSUEL

Many a man does not find his heart
until he has lost his head.

FRIEDRICH NIETZSCHE

A good heart is better than all the heads in the world.

EDWARD BULWER-LYTTON

What the heart knows today,
the head will understand tomorrow.

JAMES STEPHENS

There is no feeling in a human heart which exists in that heart
alone—which is not, in some form or degree, in every heart.

GEORGE MACDONALD

What comes from the heart, goes to the heart.

SAMUEL TAYLOR COLERIDGE

The human heart opens only to the heart
that opens in return.

MARIA EDGEWORTH

For every beauty there is an eye somewhere to see it.
For every truth there is an ear somewhere to hear it.
For every love there is a heart somewhere to receive it.

IVAN PANIN

So long as the memory of certain beloved friends
lives in my heart, I shall say that life is good.

HELEN KELLER

Absence makes the heart grow fonder.

THOMAS HAYNES BAYLY

They say absence makes the heart grow fonder,
so I figure that's why my boyfriend moved.

CHRISTY MURPHY

Love is space and time measured by the heart.

MARCEL PROUST

If you have much, give of your wealth;
if you have little, give of your heart.

ARAB PROVERB

Without a rich heart, wealth is an ugly beggar.

RALPH WALDO EMERSON

Accept the things to which fate binds you,
and love the people with whom fate brings you together,
but do so with all your heart.

MARCUS AURELIUS

If you find it in your heart to care for somebody else,
you will have succeeded.

MAYA ANGELOU

The moment you have in your heart this extraordinary thing
called love and feel the depth, the delight, the ecstasy of it,
you will discover that for you the world is transformed.

J. KRISHNAMURTI

Love wasn't put in your heart to stay,
Love isn't love till you give it away.

ANONYMOUS

A loving heart is the truest wisdom.

CHARLES DICKENS

Your heart is greater than your wounds.

HENRI J. M. NOUWEN

Nobody has ever measured, not even poets,
how much the heart can hold.

ZELDA FITZGERALD

When you begin to touch your heart or
let your heart be touched, you begin to discover that
it's bottomless, that it doesn't have any resolution,
that this heart is huge, vast, and limitless.

PEMA CHODRON

Love makes all hard hearts gentle.

GEORGE HERBERT

When the seeds of brotherly love take root
in the hearts of people, wars will cease.

PARAMAHANSA YOGANANDA

I will make love my greatest weapon and none on who I call
can defend against its force... My love will melt all hearts
liken to the sun whose rays soften the coldest day.

OG MANDINO

Keep love in your heart. A life without it is like a sunless
garden when the flowers are dead. The consciousness of
loving and being loved brings a warmth and richness to life
that nothing else can bring.

OSCAR WILDE

Occasionally in life there are those moments of unutterable fulfillment which cannot be completely explained by those symbols called words. Their meanings can only be articulated by the inaudible language of the heart.

MARTIN LUTHER KING, JR.

Give all to love; Obey thy heart.

RALPH WALDO EMERSON

**Let those love now who never loved before;
Let those who always loved, now love the more.**

THOMAS PARNELL

All the world loves a lover.

RALPH WALDO EMERSON

We are most alive when we're in love.

JOHN UPDIKE

I should like to call you by all the endearing epithets, and
yet I can find no lovelier word than the simple word "dear",
but there is a particular way of saying it. My dear one, then,
I have wept for joy to think that you are mine.

ROBERT SCHUMANN

If you love 'em in the morning with their eyes full of crust;
if you love 'em at night with their hair full of rollers,
chances are, you're in love.

MILES DAVIS

Two souls with but a single thought,
Two hearts that beat as one.

FRIEDRICH HALM

When you're in love,
it's the most glorious two-and-a-half days of your life.

RICHARD LEWIS

**If you can stay in love for more than two years,
you're on something.**

FRAN LEBOWITZ

**There is only one situation I can think of in which men and
women make an effort to read better than they usually do.
When they are in love and reading a love letter, they read for
all they are worth. They read every word three ways; they read
between the lines and in the margins.... Then, if never before
or after, they read.**

MORTIMER J. ADLER

**A love letter begins by your not knowing what you are going
to say, and ends by your not knowing what you have said.**

ANONYMOUS

**What a woman says to her lover
should be written on air or swift water.**

CATULLUS

**A woman knows the face of the man she loves
like a sailor knows the open sea.**

HONORÉ DE BALZAC

Women prefer men who have something tender about them–
especially the legal kind.

KAY INGRAM

There is a place you can touch a woman that will drive her crazy.
Her heart.

MELANIE GRIFFITH

When a young man complains that a young lady has no heart,
it is pretty certain that she has his.

GEORGE DENISON PRENTICE

Men always want to be a woman's first love—
women like to be a man's last romance.

OSCAR WILDE

One makes mistakes: that is life.
But it is never quite a mistake to have loved.

ROMAIN ROLLAND

It is better to have loved and lost,
than never to have loved at all.

ALFRED, LORD TENNYSON

If you believe yourself unfortunate,
because you have loved and lost, perish the thought.
One who has loved truly, can never lose entirely.

NAPOLEON HILL

The quarrels of lovers are like summer storms.
Everything is more beautiful when they have passed.

SUZANNE NECKER

Anyone can be passionate,
but it takes real lovers to be silly.

ROSE FRANKEN

Among those whom I like or admire, I can find no common
denominator, but among those whom I love, I can:
all of them make me laugh.

W. H. AUDEN

Lovers can live on kisses and cool water.

FRENCH PROVERB

Love and Marriage

Loving Couples

To have and to hold from this day forward,
for better for worse, for richer for poorer,
in sickness and in health, to love and to cherish,
'til death us do part.

THE BOOK OF COMMON PRAYER

Marriage is like a flourishing garden, alive with rich soil, colorful blooms, delightful fragrances and pleasant surprises— and thorns, beetles, weeds, and perhaps a mole.

NANCY McCORD

Marriage is like twirling a baton, turning a handspring or eating with chopsticks; it looks easy until you try it.

HELEN ROWLAND

Marriage is not a ritual or an end. It is a long, intricate, intimate dance together and nothing matters more than your own sense of balance and your choice of partner.

AMY BLOOM

Marriage is like pantyhose. It all depends on what you put into it.

PHYLLIS SCHLAFLY

Marriage is like a bank account. You put it in, you take it out, you lose interest.

PROFESSOR IRWIN COREY

Marriage resembles a pair of shears, so joined that they can
not be separated; often moving in opposite directions, yet
always punishing anyone who comes between them.

SYDNEY SMITH

Marriage is a woman's hair net tangled
in a man's spectacles on top of a dresser drawer.

DON HEROLD

Marriage is like vitamins:
we supplement each other's minimum daily requirements.

KATHY MOHNKE

A marriage is like a long trip in a tiny rowboat:
if one passenger starts to rock the boat, the other has to
steady it; otherwise they will go to the bottom together.

DAVID ROBERT REUBEN

Marriage is not just spiritual communion and passionate embraces; marriage is also three-meals-a-day and remembering to carry out the trash.

JOYCE BROTHERS

Marriage is a lot like the army, everyone complains, but you'd be surprised at the large number that re-enlist.

JAMES GARNER

It (marriage) may be compared to a cage, the birds without try desperately to get in, and those within try desperately to get out.

MICHEL DE MONTAIGNE

Marriage is a good deal like a circus: there is not as much in it as is represented in the advertising.

EDGAR WATSON HOWE

Marriage is a wonderful invention; but, then again,
so is a bicycle repair kit.

BILLY CONNOLLY

Marriage is our last, best chance to grow up.

JOSEPH BARTH

Coupling....Two people holding each other up like flying
buttresses. Two people depending on each other and babying
each other and defending each other against the world
outside. Sometimes it was worth all the disadvantages of
marriage just to have that: one friend in an indifferent world.

ERICA JONG

A marriage makes of two fractional lives a whole; it gives to
two purposeless lives a work, and doubles the strength of
each to perform it; it gives to two questioning natures a
reason for living, and something to live for.

MARK TWAIN

What's the best way to have your husband remember your
anniversary? Get married on his birthday.

Cindy Garner

You and your husband are alone in a cabin for the first time
since your marriage. He is nibbling on your ear. Do you
(a) nibble back or (b) tell him the toilet is running?

Erma Bombeck

Marrying a man is like buying something you've been
admiring for a long time in a shop window.
You may love it when you get it home,
but it doesn't always go with everything else.

Jean Kerr

I want a man who's kind and understanding.
Is that too much to ask of a millionaire?

Zsa Zsa Gabor

There is only one thing for a man to do who is married
to a woman who enjoys spending money,
and that is to enjoy earning it.

EDGAR WATSON HOWE

An archaeologist is the best husband any woman can have;
the older she gets, the more interested he is in her.

AGATHA CHRISTIE

My parents want me to get married. They don't care who
anymore as long as he doesn't have a pierced ear,
that's all they care about. I think men who have a pierced
ear are better prepared for marriage.
They've experienced pain and bought jewelry.

RITA RUDNER

By all means marry. If you get a good wife, you'll be happy.
If you get a bad one, you'll become a philosopher.

SOCRATES

I love being married... It's so great to find that one special
person you want to annoy for the rest of your life.

RITA RUDNER

A girl must marry for love,
and keep on marrying until she finds it.

ZSA ZSA GABOR

One good reason to get married is you'll always have
someone to blame when you can't find your keys.

JOHN LOUIS ANDERSON

I...chose my wife, as she did her wedding gown, not for a
fine glossy surface, but such qualities as would wear well.

OLIVER GOLDSMITH

People shop for a bathing suit with more care than they do a
husband or wife. The rules are the same. Look for something
you'll feel comfortable wearing. Allow for room to grow.

ERMA BOMBECK

Women hope men will change after marriage, but they don't;
men hope women won't change, but they do.

BETTINA ARNDT

What's the difference between a boyfriend and a husband?
About 30 pounds.

CINDY GARNER

Instead of getting married again, I'm going to find a woman
I don't like and just give her a house.

ROD STEWART

The real act of marriage takes place in the heart, not in the
ballroom or church or synagogue. It's a choice you make—not
just on your wedding day, but over and over again—and that
choice is reflected in the way you treat your husband or wife.

BARBARA DE ANGELIS

I would like to have engraved inside every wedding band,
"Be kind to one another." This is the golden rule of marriage
and the secret of making love last through the years.

RUDOLPH RAY

A successful marriage
is an edifice that must be rebuilt every day.

ANDRÉ MAUROIS

Remember that a good marriage is like a campfire.
Both grow cold if left unattended.

H. JACKSON BROWN, JR.

Marriages we regard as the happiest are those in which each
of the partners believes that he or she got the best of it.

SYDNEY J. HARRIS

A good marriage is at least 80 percent good luck in finding
the right person at the right time. The rest is trust.

NANETTE NEWMAN

There is no greater risk, perhaps, than matrimony,
but there is nothing happier than a happy marriage.

BENJAMIN DISRAELI

There is no more lovely, friendly and charming relationship,
communion or company than a good marriage.

MARTIN LUTHER

People are always asking couples whose marriage
has endured at least a quarter of a century for their
secret for success. Actually, it is not secret at all.
I am a forgiving woman. Long ago, I forgave my
husband for not being Paul Newman.

ERMA BOMBECK

The best thing that can happen to a couple married for fifty
years or more is that they both grow nearsighted together.

LINDA FITERMAN

One reason we lasted so long is that we usually played two
people who were very much in love. As we were realistic actors,
we became those two people. So we had a divertissement:
I had an affair with him, and he with me.

LYNN FONTANNE

Love seems the swiftest, but it is the slowest of all growths.
No man or woman really knows what perfect love is until
they have been married a quarter of a century.

MARK TWAIN

After fifteen years of marriage, my wife wants us to recommit
our vows. As a man, I don't understand her need to get
married again. We've got our toaster, let's move on.

ROBERT G. LEE

My wife, Mary, and I have been married for forty-seven
years, and not once have we had an argument serious
enough to consider divorce; murder, yes, but divorce, never.

JACK BENNY

The secret to happy marriages, relationships and terrific
friendships includes the ability to be playful and childlike.

DALE ANDERSON

Sexiness wears thin after a while, but to be married to a man who makes you laugh every day, ah, now that's a real treat.

JOANNE WOODWARD

We cannot really love anybody
with whom we never laugh.

AGNES REPPLIER

I want to make my wife laugh more.
Laughter engenders love.

RABBI SHMULEY BOTEACH

Some people ask the secret of our long marriage. We take time to go to a restaurant two times a week. A little candlelight, dinner, music and dancing. She goes Tuesdays. I go Fridays.

HENNY YOUNGMAN

Before marriage the three little words are, "I love you";
after marriage they are, "Let's eat out."

ANONYMOUS

Through all the years of my marriage, my love for Camille,
like my stomach, has steadily grown.

BILL COSBY

A good marriage is like a casserole,
only those responsible for it really know what goes in it.

ANONYMOUS

A long marriage is two people trying to dance a duet
and two solos at the same time.

ANNE TAYLOR FLEMING

♫

Marriage should be a duet—
when one sings, the other claps.

JOE MURRAY

The only thing wrong with marriage
is not seeing enough of each other.

EARL RUSSELL

A happy marriage is a long conversation
which always seems too short.

ANDRÉ MAUROIS

The wonderful thing about marriage is that
you are the most important person in someone else's life.
If you don't come home some evening, there is someone
who is going to go out looking for you.

JOYCE BROTHERS

Take each other for better or worse but not for granted.

ARLENE DAHL

Chains do not hold a marriage together. It is threads, hundreds
of tiny threads, which sew people together through the years.

SIMONE SIGNORET

Never forget the nine most important words of any marriage:
1. I love you. 2. You are beautiful. 3. Please forgive me.

H. JACKSON BROWN, JR.

The great secret of successful marriage is to treat all
disasters as incidents and none of the incidents as disasters.

HAROLD NICOLSON

The secret of a happy marriage remains a secret.

HENNY YOUNGMAN

M Is for the Million Things She Gave Me

A Mother's Love

Nothing's better than a mother's love.

AFRICAN PROVERB

There is no friendship, no love,
like that of the mother for the child.

HENRY WARD BEECHER

The greatest love is a mother's; then comes a dog's;
then comes a sweetheart's.

POLISH PROVERB

A mother's love for her child is like nothing else in the
world. It knows no law, no pity; it dares all things and
crushes down remorselessly all that stands in its path.

AGATHA CHRISTIE

A mother's love perceives no impossibilities.

BENJAMIN HENRY PADDOCK

There is no other closeness in human life
like the closeness between a mother and her baby—
chronologically, physically, and spiritually they are just
a few heartbeats away from being the same person.

SUSAN CHEEVER

A mother's heart is a baby's most beautiful dwelling.

ED DUSSAULT

Making the decision to have a child—it's momentous.
It is to decide forever to have your heart
go walking around outside your body.

ELIZABETH STONE

The heart of a mother is a deep abyss at the bottom of which
you will always find forgiveness.

HONORÉ DE BALZAC

For me, motherhood has been the one true, great, and wholly
successful romance. It is the only love I have known that is
expansive and that could have stretched to contain with
equal passion more than one object.

IRMA KURTZ

When you are a mother, you are never really alone
in your thoughts. A mother always has to think twice,
once for herself and once for her child.

SOPHIA LOREN

A mother is a person, seeing there are
only four pieces of pie for five people, who promptly
announces she never did care for pie.

TENNEVA JORDAN

I was not a classic mother. But my kids were
never palmed off to boarding school. So, I didn't bake
cookies. You can buy cookies, but you can't buy love.

RAQUEL WELCH

The mother loves her child most divinely, not when she
surrounds him with comfort and anticipates his wants, but
when she resolutely holds him to the highest standards and
is content with nothing less than his best.

HAMILTON WRIGHT MABIE

No matter how old a mother is, she still watches
her middle-aged children for signs of improvement.

Florida Scott-Maxwell

You have to love your children unselfishly.
That's hard, but it's the only way.

Barbara Bush

Can we love our children when they are homely, awkward,
unkempt, flaunting the styles and friendships we don't
approve of, when they fail to be the best, the brightest, the
most accomplished at school or even at home? Can we be
there when their world has fallen apart and only we can
restore their faith and confidence in life?

Neil Kurshan

The child who acts unlovable
is the child who most needs to be loved.

Cathy Rindner Tempelsman

A baby is born with a need to be loved—
and never outgrows it.

Frank A. Clark

The more love you give your children, the more love
you are helping them to create inside themselves.
Think of love as a basic right of your kids. Give it away
freely, and it will come back a thousand fold.

STEPHANIE MARSTON

Mother's love is peace. It need not be acquired,
it need not be deserved.

ERICH FROMM

I actually remember feeling delight,
at two o'clock in the morning, when the baby woke for
his feed, because I so longed to have another look at him.

MARGARET DRABBLE

A mother doesn't give a damn about your looks.
She thinks you are beautiful anyway.

MARION C. GARRETTY

Loving a baby is a circular business, a kind of feedback loop.
The more you give the more you get and the more you get
the more you feel like giving.

PENELOPE LEACH

**Give a little love to a child,
and you get a great deal back.**

JOHN RUSKIN

My best creation is my children.

DIANE VON FURSTENBERG

Cherishing children is the mark of a civilized society.

JOAN GANZ COONEY

**If you can't hold children in your arms,
please hold them in your heart.**

CLARA HALE

**My mother loved children—
she would have given anything if I had been one.**

GROUCHO MARX

Some are kissing mothers and some are
scolding mothers, but it is love just the same,
and most mothers kiss and scold together.

PEARL S. BUCK

The only thing worth stealing
is a kiss from a sleeping child.

JOE HOULDSWORTH

We say "I love you" to our children, but it's not enough.
Maybe that's why mothers hug and hold
and rock and kiss and pat.

JOAN MCINTOSH

Have you hugged your child today?

SLOGAN

I Can't Give You Anything but Love, Baby

Loving Yourself

I celebrate myself, and sing myself.

WALT WHITMAN

Have you hugged yourself today?

Anonymous

To love oneself is the beginning of a life-long romance.

Oscar Wilde

I feel so good that I'm going to kiss myself.

James Brown

I don't like myself, I'm crazy about myself.

Mae West

We are all worms. I believe I am a glowworm.

Winston Churchill

**The most profound relationship we'll ever have
is the one with ourselves.**

Shirley MacLaine

Without self-love it is impossible to love others.

Hermann Hesse

I continue to explain that no matter what their problem
seems to be, there is only one thing I ever work on
with anyone, and this is Loving the Self. Love is the miracle
cure. Loving ourselves works miracles in our lives.

LOUISE L. HAY

Self-love is the only weight-loss aid
that really works in the long run.

JENNY CRAIG

He who is in love with himself has at least this advantage—
he won't encounter many rivals.

GEORG CHRISTOPH LICHTENBERG

Love yourself first and everything else falls into line. You
really have to love yourself to get anything done in this world.

LUCILLE BALL

If you aren't good at loving yourself, you will have a difficult
time loving anyone, since you'll resent the time and energy you
give another person that you aren't even giving to yourself.

BARBARA DE ANGELIS

Self-love, my liege, is not so vile a sin, as self-neglecting.

WILLIAM SHAKESPEARE

**Giving love to others is directly related to
how much love you have for yourself.**

WAYNE DYER

**Self-love is not opposed to the love of other people.
You cannot really love yourself and do yourself a favor
without doing people a favor, and vice versa.**

KARL MENNINGER

**A dog is the only thing on earth
that loves you more than you love yourself.**

JOSH BILLINGS

**When you look back on your life and try to figure out where
you've been and where you are going, when you look at your
work, your love affairs, your marriages, your children, your
pain, your happiness—when you examine all that closely,
what you really find out is that the only person you really go
to bed with is yourself.**

SHIRLEY MacLAINE

**Know yourself. Don't accept your dog's admiration
as conclusive evidence that you are wonderful.**

ANN LANDERS

Seek not outside yourself, heaven is within.

MARY LOU COOK

**You can explore the universe looking for somebody who
is more deserving of your love and affection than you are
yourself, and you will not find that person anywhere.**

BUDDHIST SAYING

**Love is based first of all on developing the love of one's life
within. Rather than looking for Mr. or Ms. Right out there,
it's *becoming* Mr. or Ms. Right.**

HAROLD BLOOMFIELD

**The ability to love oneself, combined with the ability
to love life, fully accepting that it won't last forever,
enables one to improve the quality of life.**

BERNIE SIEGEL

A loving person lives in a loving world. A hostile person lives in a hostile world: everyone you meet is your mirror.

KEN KEYES, JR.

My true relationship is my relationship with myself—
all others are simply mirrors of it. As I learn to love myself,
I automatically receive the love and appreciation
from others that I desire.

SHAKTI GAWAIN

Don't forget to love yourself.

SØREN KIERKEGAARD

End your day by privately looking directly into your eyes
in the mirror and saying, "I love you." Do this for thirty
days and watch how you transform.

MARK VICTOR HANSEN

I'd date me!

BRAD PITT

Embraceable You
Hugs and Kisses

In the coldest February,
as in every month in every other year,
the best thing we can hold onto is each other.

LINDA ELLERBEE

They invented hugs to let people know you love them
without saying anything.

BIL KEANE

A silent hug means a thousand words
to the unhappy heart.

ANONYMOUS

Sometimes it's better to put love into hugs
than to put it into words.

ANONYMOUS

Nine times out of ten, when you extend your arms
to someone, they will step in, because basically
they need precisely what you need.

LEO BUSCAGLIA

Millions and millions of years would still
not give me half enough time to describe
that tiny instant of all eternity when you put your
arms around me and I put my arms around you.

JACQUES PRÉVERT

You can't wrap love in a box,
but you can wrap a person in a hug.

ANONYMOUS

Oh, I love hugging. I wish I was an octopus,
so I could hug 10 people at a time!

DREW BARRYMORE

A hug is a handshake from the heart.

ANONYMOUS

A hug is a smile with arms,
a laugh with a stronger grip.

TERRI GUILLEMETS

A career is a wonderful thing,
but you can't snuggle up to it on a cold night.

MARILYN MONROE

No matter how hard you hug your money,
it never hugs back.

H. JACKSON BROWN, JR.

Everyone wants a hug and kiss.
It translates into any language.

GEORGETTE MOSBACHER

Offer hugs, not drugs.

ADINA LEBOWITZ

Arm ourselves for war?
No! All the arms we need are for hugging.

ANONYMOUS

A hug is like a boomerang—you get it back right away.

BIL KEANE

An emotional hug can be a thinking-of-you letter,
a thank-you card, or a phone call.

DAVID DENOTARIS

If you're angry at a loved one, hug that person. And mean it. You may not want to hug—which is all the more reason to do so. It's hard to stay angry when someone shows they love you, and that's precisely what happens when we hug each other.

WALTER ANDERSON

Hugging has no unpleasant side effects and is all natural. There are no batteries to replace, it's inflation-proof and non-fattening with no monthly payments. It's non-taxable, non-polluting, and is, of course, fully refundable.

ANONYMOUS

Hug Department. Always Open.

ANONYMOUS

Kiss, n. A word invented by the poets as a rhyme for "bliss".

AMBROSE BIERCE

A kiss is a lovely trick designed by nature to stop speech
when words become superfluous.

INGRID BERGMAN

The most eloquent silence:
that of two mouths meeting in a kiss.

ANONYMOUS

There is the kiss of welcome and of parting;
the long, lingering, loving, present one; the stolen,
or the mutual one; the kiss of love, of joy, and of sorrow;
the seal of promise and receipt of fulfillment.

THOMAS C. HALIBURTON

A thing of no use to one, but prized by two.

ROBERT ZWICKEY

A pleasant reminder that two heads are better than one.

REX PROUTY

A kiss is strange. It's a living thing, a communication,
a whole wild emotion expressed in a simple moist touch.

MICKEY SPILLANE

A kiss can be a comma, a question mark, or an exclamation
point. That's basic spelling that every woman ought to know.

MISTINGUETTE

A kiss is something you cannot give without taking
and cannot take without giving.

ANONYMOUS

A kiss is like singing into someone's mouth.

DIANE ACKERMAN

'Tis a secret
Told to the mouth instead of to the ear

EDMOND ROSTAND

Kisses are the messengers of love.

DANISH PROVERB

A kiss is a rosy dot over the "I" of loving.

Cyrano de Bergerac

**Kisses are like grains of gold or silver
found upon the ground, of no value themselves,
but precious as showing that a mine is near.**

George Villiers

**Kissing is a means of getting two people so close together
that they can't see anything wrong with each other.**

Gene Yasenak

Kissing is our greatest invention.

Tom Robbins

People who throw kisses are hopelessly lazy.

Bob Hope

**Any man who can drive safely while kissing a pretty girl
is simply not giving the kiss the attention it deserves.**

Albert Einstein

The doctor must have put (my pacemaker) in wrong.
Every time my husband kisses me, the garage door goes up.

MINNIE PEARL

We did one of those quick, awkward kisses where each of you
gets a nose in the eye.

CLIVE JAMES

I don't know how to kiss, or I would kiss you.
Where do the noses go?

INGRID BERGMAN IN *FOR WHOM THE BELL TOLLS*

A kiss without a mustache is like an egg without salt.

SPANISH PROVERB

Q: Does your wife mind kissing you with that beard?
A: Not at all. She's happy to go through a forest to
    get to a picnic.

ARCHIE MOORE

I wasn't kissing her. I was whispering in her mouth.

CHICO MARX

...let us kiss each other's eyes, And laugh our love away.

WILLIAM BUTLER YEATS

I'd love to kiss you, but I just washed my hair.

BETTE DAVIS IN *CABIN IN THE COTTON*

**Kisses may not spread germs,
but they certainly lower resistance.**

LOUISE ERICKSON

Is kissing dirty? Only if you do it right.

WOODY ALLEN

A kiss without a hug is like a flower without the fragrance.

PROVERB

Anyone who's a great kisser I'm always interested in.

CHER

I have found men who didn't know how to kiss.
I've always found time to teach them.

MAE WEST

I kissed my first girl and smoked my first cigarette on the
same day. I haven't had time for tobacco since.

ARTURO TOSCANINI

Four sweet lips, two pure souls, and one undying affection—
these are love's pretty ingredients for a kiss.

CHRISTIAN NESTELL BOVEE

In love there is always one who kisses,
and the other who offers the cheek.

FRENCH PROVERB

What I like about France is the kissing—
one of civilization's finest achievements.

ISABEL HUGGAN

May we kiss whom we please
And please whom we kiss.

ANONYMOUS

Kiss till the cow comes home.

FRANCIS BEAUMONT

Drink to me only with thine eyes,
And I will pledge with mine;
Or leave a kiss within the cup,
And I'll not look for wine.

BEN JONSON

Give me a thousand kisses and yet more;
And then repeat those that have gone before.

ANONYMOUS

One kiss more, and so farewell.

ANONYMOUS

Kissing power is stronger than will power.

ABIGAIL VAN BUREN

Then I did the simplest thing in the world. I leaned down...and kissed him. And the world cracked open.

AGNES DE MILLE

We kiss, and it feels like we have just shrugged off the world.

JIM SHANHIN

With a kiss let us set out for an unknown world.

ALFRED DE MUSSET

My child, if you finally decide to let a man kiss you, put your whole heart and soul into it. No man likes to kiss a rock.

LADY CHESTERFIELD

I believe in long, slow, deep, soft, wet kisses
that last for three days.

KEVIN COSTNER IN *BULL DURHAM*

A kiss must last long to be enjoyed.

GREEK PROVERB

The kiss you take is better than you give.

WILLIAM SHAKESPEARE

Stolen kisses are always sweetest.

LEIGH HUNT

A legal kiss is never as good as a stolen one.

GUY DE MAUPASSANT

Stealing a kiss may be petty larceny
but sometimes it's also grand.

ANONYMOUS

Be plain in dress, and sober in your diet;
In short, my deary, kiss me, and be quiet.

MARY WORTLEY MONTAGU

For it was not into my ear you whispered, but into my heart.
It was not my lips you kissed, but my soul.

JUDY GARLAND

Soul meet soul on lovers' lips.

PERCY BYSSHE SHELLEY

He kisses me and now I am someone else; someone else in
the pulse that repeats the pulse of my own veins and in the
breath that mingles with my breath.

GABRIELA MISTRAL

...how she felt when first he kissed her—like a tub of roses
swimming in honey, cologne, nutmeg, and blackberries.

SAMUEL SULLIVAN COX

When she kissed him,
he melted like a lump of milk chocolate.

MARGE PIERCY

We turned on one another deep, drowned gazes, and exchanged
a kiss that reduced my bones to rubber and my brain to
gruel.

PETER DE VRIES

The sound of a kiss is not so loud as that of a cannon,
but its echo lasts a great deal longer.

OLIVER WENDELL HOLMES

Love Potion Number Nine

Love Conquers All

One word frees us of all the weight and pain of life:
that word is love.

Sophocles

Love comforteth like sunshine after rain.

WILLIAM SHAKESPEARE

**Love cures people—both the ones who give it
and the ones who receive it.**

KARL MENNINGER

**Our ability to pray for people and surround them with love
makes an enormous difference in how they feel and heal.**

PEGGY HUDDLESTON

**This is the miracle that happens every time to those who
really love: the more they give, the more they possess of that
precious nourishing love from which flowers and children
have their strength and which could help all human beings
if they would take it without doubting.**

RAINER MARIA RILKE

We can look for every opportunity to give and receive love,
to appreciate nature, to heal our wounds
and the wounds of others,
to forgive, and to serve.

JOAN BORYSENKO

One cannot be strong without love.
For love is not an irrelevant emotion; it is the blood of life,
the power of reunion with the separated.

PAUL TILLICH

If grass can grow through cement,
love can find you at every time in your life.

CHER

Love is a force more formidable than any other. It is invisible—
it cannot be seen or measured, yet it is powerful enough
to transform you in a moment, and offer you more joy
than any material possession could.

BARBARA DE ANGELIS

There is no difficulty that enough love will not conquer, no disease that enough love will not heal, no door that enough love will not bridge, no wall that enough love will not throw down, no sin that enough love will not redeem.... It makes no difference how deeply seated may be the trouble, how hopeless the outlook, how muddled the tangle, how great the mistake. A sufficient realization of love will dissolve it all. If only you could love enough, you could be the happiest and most powerful being in the world...

EMMET FOX

Love, and love alone,
is capable of giving thee a happier life.

LUDWIG VON BEETHOVEN

The cure for all ills and wrongs, the cares, the sorrows and the crimes of humanity, all lie in the one word "love." It is the divine that everywhere produces and restores life.

LYDIA MARIA CHILD

Love and food are equally vital
to our sanity and survival.

KUO TZU

Love is the only sane and satisfactory answer
to the problems of human existence.

ERICH FROMM

Love is the key to the solution of the problems of the world.

MARTIN LUTHER KING, JR.

Love alone is capable of uniting living beings in such a way
as to complete and fulfill them, for it alone takes them and
joins them by what is deepest in themselves.

PIERRE TEILHARD DE CHARDIN

Then I grasped the meaning of the greatest secret that
human poetry and human thought and belief have to impart:
The salvation of man is through love and in love.

VIKTOR FRANKL

If you have love in your life it can make up for a great many
things that are missing. If you don't have love in your life,
no matter what else there is, it's not enough.

ANN LANDERS

Under the sustaining influence of love,
the physical body is always at its best.
It is probably true that more people are sick
from lack of love in their lives
than from all other causes put together.

ERIC BUTTERWORTH

Age does not protect you from love.
But love, to some extent, protects you from age.

JEANNE MOREAU

Where there is love there is life.

MAHATMA GANDHI

Treasure the love you receive above all.
It will survive long after your good health has vanished.

OG MANDINO

Kiss the place to make it well.

ANN TAYLOR

Where love reigns the impossible may be attained.

INDIAN PROVERB

It is love, not faith, that removes mountains.

GEORGE SAND

When I despair, I remember that all through history the way
of truth and love has always won. There have been tyrants
and murderers and for a time they seem invincible
but in the end, they always fall—Think of it, ALWAYS.

MAHATMA GANDHI

Love accomplishes all things.

FRANCESCO PETRARCH

Darkness cannot drive out darkness; only light can do that.
Hate cannot drive out hate: only love can do that.

MARTIN LUTHER KING, JR.

There is a single magic, a single power, a single salvation,
and a single happiness, and that is called loving.

HERMANN HESSE

Love is one of the most powerful energies of the universe.
It is thousands of times stronger than anger, resentment or fear.

SANAYA ROMAN

Love builds bridges where there are none.

R. H. DELANEY

Love creates an "us"
without destroying the "me."

LEO BUSCAGLIA

We do not judge the people we love.

JEAN-PAUL SARTRE

**To love deeply in one direction
makes us more loving in all others.**

ANNE-SOPHIE SWETCHINE

**Love's greatest gift is its ability
to make everything it touches sacred.**

BARBARA DE ANGELIS

**Love and you will be loved, and you will be able to do
all that you could not do unloved.**

MARQUÉS DE SANTILLANA

**Love is the only force capable
of transforming an enemy into a friend.**

MARTIN LUTHER KING, JR.

Where there is great love,
there are always miracles.

WILLA CATHER

When the power of love becomes more important than the
love of power, then will there be peace.

JIMI HENDRIX

All You Need Is Love

Unconditional Love

Love is all we have,
the only way that each can help the other.

EURIPIDES

**Never waste an opportunity
to tell someone you love them.**

H. JACKSON BROWN, JR.

If you judge people, you have no time to love them.

MOTHER TERESA

**Don't look for love; give love—
and you will find love looking for you.**

BETH BLACK

Teach only love for that is what you are.

A COURSE IN MIRACLES

**Close the door when you get home from work, and hug and
kiss with someone special for at least fifteen minutes—
longer is better.**

ANITA BAKER

**Don't make love by the garden gate,
love is blind but the neighbors ain't.**

ANONYMOUS

Never succumb to the temptation of becoming bitter.
As you press for justice, be sure to move with dignity
and discipline, using only the weapon of Love.

MARTIN LUTHER KING, JR.

Do not seek perfection in a changing world.
Instead, perfect your love.

BUDDHA

We can forgive as long as we love.

FRANÇOIS DUC DE LA ROCHEFOUCAULD

Do all things with love.

OG MANDINO

What the world really needs
is more love and less paperwork.

PEARL BAILEY

Love is more important than your precious image. Love is more important than money. Love is more important than rules. Love is more important than being right. Love is more important than efficiency. Love is more important than sleep. Love is more important than sex. Love is more important than being on time. Love is more important than getting your own way. Love is more important than the taste of food. Love is more important than people meeting your models. Love is more important than your plans. Love is more important than having time alone. Love is more important than your success. Love is more important than your health. Love is more important than your pride of prestige. Love is more important than having a skinny figure. Love is more important than anything else.

KEN KEYES, JR.

True love is unconquerable and irresistible.
It goes on gathering power and spreading itself,
until eventually it transforms everyone whom it touches.

MEHER BABA

True love is that which ennobles the personality,
fortifies the heart, and sanctifies the existence.

HENRI FRÉDÉRIC AMIEL

When souls really touch, it is forever.
Then space and time disappear, and all that remains
is the consciousness that we are not alone in life.

JOAN CHITTISTER

When we are motivated by goals that have deep meaning,
by dreams that need completion, by pure love that needs
expressing, then we truly live life.

GREG ANDERSON

Perfect love is rare indeed—for to be a lover will require that you continually have the subtlety of the very wise, the flexibility of the child, the sensitivity of the artist, the understanding of the philosopher, the acceptance of the saint, the tolerance of the scholar and the fortitude of the certain.

LEO BUSCAGLIA

Perfect love sometimes does not come
till the first grandchild.

WELSH PROVERB

When we find someone whose weirdness is compatible with ours, we join up with them and fall into mutually satisfying weirdness—and call it love—true love.

ROBERT FULGHUM

We don't believe in rheumatism and true love
until after the first attack.

MARIE VON EBNER-ESCHENBACH

True love begins
when nothing is asked for it in return.

ANTOINE DE SAINT EXUPÉRY

True love comes quietly, without banners or flashing lights.
If you hear bells, get your ears checked.

ERICH SEGAL

If only one could tell true love from false love as one can tell
mushrooms from toadstools.

KATHERINE MANSFIELD

Our basic nature is incredible wisdom and unconditional love.
All we have to do is peel away the layers of beliefs and condi-
tioning collectively called the ego, which prevent the light of our
own true nature from shining forth.

JOAN BORYSENKO

There isn't anyone you couldn't love once you've heard their story.

MARY LOU KOWNACKI

Discovering an ability to love uncritically and totally has been
exhilarating. It's the sort of love that calls upon my whole being,
bringing all of my potential to life.

RONNIE FRIEDLAND

When we learn to love and serve everyone unconditionally,
we begin to experience that life is a cornucopia
which gives us far more security, sensations and
power than we really need to be happy.

KEN KEYES, JR. AND BRUCE BURKAN

Love and concern for all are not things some of us are born
with and others are not. Rather, they are results of what we
do with our minds: We can choose to transform our minds
so that they embody love, or we can allow them to develop
habits and false concepts of separation.

SHARON SALZBERG

Unconditional love is the most powerful stimulant
to the immune system.

BERNIE SIEGEL

Love everybody and don't let flags and religions
get in the way of looking somebody in the eye
and seeing the beauty of the human person.

MAIRCEÁD CORRIGAN

Unconditional love is loving your kids for who they are, not for what they do.... I don't mean that we like or accept inappropriate behavior, but with unconditional love we love the children even at those times when we dislike their behavior. Unconditional love isn't something you will achieve every minute of every day. But it is the thought we must hold in our hearts every day.

STEPHANIE MARSTON

The ultimate lesson all of us have to learn is unconditional love, which includes not only others but ourselves as well.

ELISABETH KÜBLER-ROSS

Love is a state of being in which
one is aware of the unity of all life.

RICHARD CHAMBERLAIN

I think I have discovered the highest good.
It is love. This principle stands at the center of the cosmos.

MARTIN LUTHER KING, JR.

The final word is love.

DOROTHY DAY

Index to Authors

L

Lafayette, Marquis de **47**

Landers, Ann **42, 91, 114**

Lao-Tzu **23**

Leach, Penelope **84**

Lebowitz, Adina **96**

Lebowitz, Fran **36, 60**

Lee, Robert G. **74**

LeGuin, Ursula **37**

Levenson, Sam **48**

Lewis, Richard **59**

Lewis, Sinclair **27**

Lichtenberg, Georg Christoph **89**

Lindbergh, Anne Morrow **31**

Longfellow, Henry Wadsworth **37, 49**

Loren, Sophia **82**

Luther, Martin **72**

M

Mabie, Hamilton Wright **82**

Macdonald, George **53**

MacLaine, Shirley **88, 90**

Mandino, Og **57, 115, 121**

Mansfield, Katherine **125**

Marquis, Don **46**

Marston, Stephanie **84, 127**

Marx, Chico **102**

Marx, Groucho **51, 85**

Maupassant, Guy de **106**

Maurois, André **72, 77**

McCord, Nancy **64**

McIntosh, Joan **86**

McKuen, Rod **40, 50**

McLaughlin, Magnon **33**

Mencken, H. L. **36**

Menninger, Karl **90, 110**

ABOUT THE AUTHOR

Allen Klein is an award-winning professional speaker, best-selling author, and the President of the Association for Applied and Therapeutic Humor (www.aath.org). He teaches people worldwide how to use humor to deal with not-so-funny stuff. In addition to this book, Klein is also the author of *Up Words for Down Days, The Change-Your-Life Quote Book, The Lift-Your-Spirits Quote Book, The Celebrate-Your-Life Quote Book, The Simplify-Your-Life Book,* and *The Wise and Witty Quote Book*, among others.

For more information about Klein or his presentations go to www.allenklein.com, e-mail him at humor@allenklein.com, or write him at 1034 Page Street, San Francisco, CA 94117.